WHEN YOUR CHILD
IS HYPERACTIVE

*New Ways to Cope with ADHD
in Your Family*

Dr. David B. Hawkins, ACSW, Ph.D.

"Feelings are real and legitimate; children behave and misbehave for a reason, even if adults cannot figure it out."

—U<small>NKNKOWN</small>

Victor is an imprint of
Cook Communications Ministries, Colorado Springs, Colorado 80918
Cook Communications, Paris, Ontario
Kingsway Communications, Eastbourne, England

WHEN YOUR CHILD IS HYPERACTIVE
© 2001 by David B. Hawkins

ISBN: 0-78143-738-5
First Printing, 2001
Printed in the United States of America

Editors: Craig Bubeck, John Conaway
Cover & Interior Design: Global Images and iDesignEtc.

ABOUT THE AUTHOR

A licensed clinical psychologist trained in the fields of social work and clinical psychology, Dr. David B. Hawkins, ACSW, Ph.D., has been in private practice for more than twenty years and specializes in domestic violence, adult and family issues, and marriage enrichment. Based in Longview, Washington, he is a certified domestic violence perpetrator treatment provider, certified forensic examiner, and a spiritual director. He also is a member of the National Association of Social Workers, Academy of Forensic Examiners, and the American Psychological Association. The author of several other books, including *See Dick and Jane Grow Up* (ISBN: 0-78143-498-X), David

has co-hosted a weekly radio broadcast entitled "Right Where You Live," was the host of an award-winning television program entitled "Community Forum," and writes a monthly column for the *Longview Daily News* entitled "Matters of the Heart."

INTRODUCTION

It was only 10:15 on a Tuesday morning when the telephone rang with a call for Mrs. Terry Smith. Terry wasn't sure she wanted to answer. She hoped that it wasn't the school again. A call came from her son's school about this time every day lately. They were only a few months into the new school year, and yet it appeared that things would be going about as they had the year before.

Reluctantly, Terry picked up the receiver and said hello. The teacher placing the call was professional, almost cold. But after a few moments, the voice on the other end of the line warmed. He apologized for the phone call, but sounded less than sincere. Clearly he was exasperated and hated making the phone call as much as she hated receiving it.

He launched into a tirade of misbehavior. "Jake is out of control, Mrs. Smith. He is slapping other kids, throwing things around the classroom, and telling me he is not going to do his work. I can't get him to stay on task." He ended by squarely placing responsibility on Mr. and Mrs. Smith to "do something" about Jake. "Have you thought about getting him some counseling and medications?"

Frustrated and angry, Terry retorted abruptly, "What do you

want me to do? Aren't you getting paid to manage him and teach him something? We have a good family and I don't think he needs any drugs!"

"Mrs. Smith," he said sternly. "We can't teach Jake anything when we have to spend all of our time keeping him in control. He's going to have to leave school again today. We can have a meeting later to decide what to do with him."

"I'll be there in a few minutes. But, I'm not happy about this," Terry replied.

It seems that Jake had been highly disruptive in the classroom, to the point where the teacher felt that the learning of the other students was being jeopardized. Not only that, Terry learned that on this particular morning Jake had gotten into a fight with another student, and it appeared to be at his instigation. In fact, the teacher later shared his concern that Jake was sometimes so aggressive he could be a danger to other students.

Terry had received dozens of calls like this one over the past few years. As a second grader Jake's schooling had never gone smoothly. She and her husband, Michael, had one other child, Todd, who was a first grader, and seemed to have none of these behavior problems. Terry and Michael had spent hours trying to understand the problem. More often than not, however, they felt stuck in anger and frustration with their son. Though they hated to admit it, they had sometimes grown weary of Jake, and wondered why he could not be more like Todd. In their darkest moments, like during another phone call from the school, Terry even felt that she did not like her son. He caused her so much inconvenience, and often her life was disrupted by his seemingly unnecessary, unruly behavior.

It was not just unruly behavior, however, that bothered Terry and Michael. It was also his refusal to follow instructions, his unfinished assignments, and a restlessness that irritated them consistently. They had worked with Jake on these traits, but he did not seem to learn from his problems. He kept repeating his disruptive behaviors in spite of their warnings, anger, and discipline. Nothing seemed to work.

Terry angrily went to the school and picked up Jake. She tried to control her anger and vowed to listen to his side of the story before making any judgments. She always found this hard to do, since his behavior simply did not make sense to her. After all, Todd was able to learn from his behavior, follow the rules, and behave like a "normal" young child. Jake was different, and the Smiths wondered what it was about them that made him behave the way he did. As she listened to Jake minimize his behavior, and blame others for his problems, she felt the same anger she had felt so many times before. She knew, however, that arguing with him would be fruitless.

When her husband arrived home that evening they decided that it was time to consult with some others about the problem. Their family life and marital relationship were being affected, Todd did not like his brother, Jake's grades and social skills were plummeting, and there was no hope on the horizon. They did not know where to turn. They agreed that they would talk to both their physician and the school psychologist.

EARLY WARNING SIGNS

Thankfully we are learning more about Attention Deficit Hyperactivity Disorder, or Attention Deficit Disorder without hyperactivity. Still, there are many lingering myths and misunderstandings, which make an early diagnosis and intervention critical. **Your Pocket Therapist** will help you understand ADHD/ADD and the impact it may be having on your family.

Attention Deficit Hyperactivity Disorder (ADHD) has been identified as a problem for many years. At times it has received the positive, concerned attention it warrants. Other times, however, it has received confusing and negative press coverage. "Kids are being drugged unnecessarily," the headlines read. "Normal kids are being sedated," others say. "Ritalin will kill you, and you'd better watch out for it. It's just the pharmaceutical companies trying to make money off our kids."

While there may have been a grain of truth to some of these allegations, by and large they are unfounded and sensationalistic, and thus cause more harm than good. Finding accurate information is hard, but critical. Again, **Your Pocket Therapist** will help you sort out fact from fiction.

Necessity of Early Intervention

It is common for parents with concerns about their children to be told that their child's behavior is "normal" and they are just "active children." Sometimes this is true, while at other times this unfortunate advice thwarts early intervention.

We now know that ADHD can be diagnosed quite early, often as early as preschool. Obviously the trained clinician will determine whether the child's behavior is "normal" and whether the family environment plays a role in the child's behavior. The clinician will also make appropriate referrals to other professionals.

> "People must help one another; it is nature's law."
>
> —*Jean De La Fontaine*

But what is the result of missed opportunities at early intervention? Research now shows that children with missed interventions are at higher risk for drug and alcohol abuse, teen pregnancies, as well as antisocial behaviors. It is commonly understood that once these symptom clusters become established they can be hard to treat. *Thus, again, early intervention is critical.*

A PLEA FOR HELP

By the time they had arranged a meeting with Jake's teacher and school psychologist, the Smiths were frazzled. The problems had been escalating and their patience was growing thin. They blamed Jake for not controlling himself and acting like the "young man" who characterized their family. It was hard not to have personal feelings about the way he often acted. They cycled through feelings of inadequacy, guilt, anger, and discouragement. They often wondered what they were doing wrong to create such a problem. All the self-help books on child discipline seemed of little value. They were repeatedly referred to books about willful children.

The school called to tell them an appointment had been scheduled. School personnel felt that they could no longer tolerate Jake's behavior. After thoroughly discussing Jake's classroom behavior, and confirming that his behavior in the home was not much better, they decided that a medical and psychological work-up were in order. They all agreed that Jake's behavior was not improving and action needed to be taken. They discussed the observed behaviors and the various explanations for them. All parties involved viewed Jake's behavior in a similar way, and this again confirmed the presence of a serious problem.

While somewhat daunting, the Smiths found the triage of discussion about Jake to be helpful. They had finally found a group of listening ears, professionals ready to take whatever action was necessary to remedy the problem. The team of professionals made numerous observations about Jake.

They noted the following concerns:

- an inability to stay on task in the classroom;
- immaturity with his peers and lack of social skills;
- acting without considering consequences;
- failure to plan ahead;
- petty stealing;
- fidgety behavior;
- disruptive behavior in the classroom;
- an insensitivity to others' needs;
- a questionable degree of remorse for misbehavior.

The team also noted many positive qualities about Jake. They noted that he often sought out attention, which in many ways meant that he strived to please others. He seemed to really long for acceptance by his peers, but did not seem to know how to get it. He had a lot of creativity and could also be very charming. One teacher found that she liked Jake at times and could see a lot of potential in him. She did not think that intelligence was the issue in his falling grades, but rather lack of motivation, organizational ability, and attention.

The team developed an additional plan from that meeting. They decided that they would have him tested by the school psychologist and medically evaluated by their pediatrician. The Smiths were encouraged not to take Jake's behavior personally as there could be a lot of plausible explanations for his behavior. That was when they first heard about Attention Deficit Hyperactivity Disorder. They had never heard that term before, but had heard the term "hyperactive." There were other possibilities to be considered as well, including other biochemical disorders, depression, and emotional issues. For the first time in years the Smiths felt that they were not alone and had a sense of direction. They set up the testing with the school psychologist that day, and planned to set up a meeting with their physician in the next few days. Finally, they felt a sense of hope and some relief.

"ONE GOOD SCHOOLMASTER IS WORTH A THOUSAND PRIESTS."

—*Robert G. Ingersoll*

Referral to the School Psychologist

As the appointment with the psychologist drew closer, both Terry and Michael found themselves feeling apprehensive. Although they wanted and needed answers, they were also fearful about what the psychologist might reveal. Would the finger of blame be pointed at them? Were they inadequate in some way? What if they had been doing things completely wrong for years and had caused irreparable harm? They reviewed together, and alone, all the mistakes they had made with Jake, wondering if these had caused all of his problems. These thoughts and impossible questions pelted their sagging confidence.

They also wondered if Jake's problems would reveal underlying issues in their family. Perhaps they had been too harsh with him, or had given their other son preferential treatment.

They felt a little shame that they had to seek the help of a professional and could not resolve the problem themselves. They read the books, were intelligent people, and were highly motivated to try every tool available. It took more courage on their part to seek help than they expected.

Jake, too, resisted the visit to the "shrink." He had known other kids who had to see the school psychologist and remembered that they had been questioned and teased by some other students. He feared that the same would happen to him. He begged his parents not to make him go to see the psychologist or doctor. He promised, as he had many times before, that he would improve his behavior. He cried, screamed, and tried every way he knew to manipulate his parents out of their plan. It almost worked. Terry and Michael continued to wonder if they were doing the right thing.

Finally Jake agreed to cooperate. After some initial hesitation and manipulation, he went for his appointment. His initial visit was difficult as Jake was more anxious than usual, exacerbating his ADHD issues. But the trained psychologist had seen this kind of behavior many times before and was able to work constructively with Jake at his pace. They developed a rapport with one another—setting the stage for testing.

Testing is a critical component of making an accurate diagnosis. Remember, *early detection, diagnosis, and intervention are extremely critical with this disorder.* The psychologist used a variety of test instruments, but most critical were a set of behavior-rating scales measuring Jake's behavior. Comparisons were made from different individuals in different settings to determine if there were any consistencies. These ratings were analyzed to determine if there were constellations of behavior meeting the criteria for ADHD or ADD.

After Jake completed a battery of tests, the Smiths were called in to review the findings. The psychologist had both good news and bad news to give to the Smiths. Standard educational testing had revealed that Jake performed well on the intellectual portions of the test, showing that he had above average capabilities to learn. He was able to master new tasks easily, and was capable of performing much higher on classroom assignments than he had been doing. The testing further revealed that he was functioning below grade level in several areas, but this seemed not to be related to capability. Rather, the psychologist suggested, it had to do with his distractibility and concentration problems. Jake struggled to maintain focus during extended phases of the testing, which correlated with his difficulties in the classroom as well.

After discussing these results with the Smiths they all agreed that further testing might be helpful. A clinical psychologist could look for emotional issues stemming from the educational deficits Jake experienced, as well as explore any social maladjustment. It was also agreed that they would have Jake evaluated by a physician for other physical factors that might effect attention and concentration.

REFERRAL TO THE CLINICAL PSYCHOLOGIST

Just as it had taken some effort to get Jake to the school psychologist, it took some coaxing to get him to cooperate with further evaluation by a clinical psychologist. The family had many discussions before confirming this decision. Jake would see Dr. Hanson, the man referred to them by the school psychologist.

Dr. Hanson's first step was to build a rapport with Jake so that he would cooperate. Jake naturally put up some initial resistance, testing a few of the boundaries set by the psychologist.

He wandered all over the psychologist's office, touching things that were defined as off limits, and becoming angry when his efforts were frustrated. This new setting, with new boundaries and expectations, created a situation where Jake was more anxious than usual. Combined with his ADHD, he was rendered fidgety, inattentive, and somewhat oppositional. In addition to the testing, these behaviors were helpful in making a tentative diagnosis.

Part of the testing offered to Jake included gaining information on how Jake behaved at home and at school. His behavior in various environments, with different stimuli, was observed. Past school performances were evaluated in light of his current functioning. These comparisons were collected and correlated with the other test data. A thorough history was taken including a developmental history. Critical questions concerning the beginning of the problematic behavior were examined. Jake's behavior in the test situation was also included in the evaluation process.

Dr. Hanson reviewed the test data, the observations by parents and teachers, and his own impressions. He considered the **primary symptoms** to include Jake's fidgety nature, distractibility, oppositional behavior, and an inability to sustain attention or remain on task. These behaviors seemed to cause him to have trouble in most typical learning situations, as well as causing social problems. These problem behaviors seemed to be escalating and growing worse. Clearly some kind of intervention was necessary.

As they had feared, Dr. Hanson also wanted to talk to the Smiths about how their family functioned. Already feeling guilty, they assumed they were going to be blamed for Jake's behavior. It would not take much to discourage them. They already second-guessed many of their interventions with Jake. They knew that in many ways they preferred to be around Todd rather than spend time managing Jake's behavior.

When Terry and Michael were asked to give a history of Jake's behavior, Terry erupted with her feelings:

"Jake demands all of my attention. If it's not one thing, it's another. I can't rest or else I'll be picking up the pieces of something he has gotten into that is off limits. At first we thought that he was just going through the Terrible Twos. Then we thought it was drifting into the Terrible Threes. We thought we had a 'willful child' on our hands. But then we moved into the Terrible Fours, Fives, and so on. It just hasn't stopped. I have to watch him every minute of the day, and it's exhausting. I don't know how much more I can take."

Next Michael shared his perspective:

"It hasn't been as hard on me as it has been on Terry, since she's with him a lot more. He is *not* a normal kid, that's for sure. He will not follow directions and does not seem to learn from past mistakes. We go over and over things with him. We know he is not stupid, but sometimes we wonder just what is going on. He gets into my tools when I've told him they are off limits. We have to lock areas that we want left alone. I hate to admit it but we've even locked him in his room so that he would not get into things and we could have some peace. A family should not have to live this way."

Terry and Michael left Dr. Hanson's office with mixed feelings. While he reassured them of many things they were doing right, it would be a while before they heard his final opinion. An appointment was set up for ten days away when they would review his findings. That would feel like an eternity to them.

After careful review of his evaluation, Dr. Hanson called the Smiths to arrange a meeting to discuss the results. At that meeting he told them that he thought Jake was struggling with a number of remediable issues. **First**, he thought that the evidence strongly pointed to Jake's having Attention Deficit Hyperactivity Disorder. **Second**, he believed that Jake had struggled with this problem for so long that he now had some significant educational deficits that would need some specialized attention. **Third**, Jake now seemed to struggle with self-esteem

"FOR THE LORD GIVES WISDOM,
AND FROM HIS MOUTH COME
KNOWLEDGE AND UNDERSTANDING."

—*Proverbs 2:6*

Understanding

problems. He seemed to have some sense that he was different and was unable to manage his behavior as was expected of him. **Fourth**, Dr. Hanson noted some of the social immaturity, peer problems, and family tension that seemed to result from Jake's difficulties. **Finally**, Dr. Hanson wanted Jake to be seen by his pediatrician and possibly a child psychiatrist. They would confirm that there were no other complicating physical problems taking place.

The Smiths were confused and yet relieved by Dr. Hanson's report. There was, at last, some possible explanation for Jake's behavior. They were also relieved to hear that there were steps that could be taken to remedy many of his problems. First, however, the Smiths needed to learn more to understand about Attention Deficit Hyperactivity Disorder.

ATTENTION DEFICIT HYPER-ACTIVITY DISORDER

What exactly is Attention Deficit Hyperactivity Disorder? In simple terms, Attention Deficit Hyperactivity Disorder (ADHD) is a developmentally inappropriate poor attention span, and often features symptoms of hyperactivity and impulsivity. Of course, as with other dysfunctions, there are a variety of manifestations of this problem including attention span problems without hyperactivity.

The American Psychiatric Association's Diagnostic and Statistical Manual of Mental Disorders (Fourth Edition, 1994) states that eight of the following criteria must have been present for at least six months to render the diagnosis of ADHD:

- often fidgets with hands or feet or squirms in seat
- has difficulty remaining seated when required to do so
- is easily distracted by extraneous stimuli
- has difficulty awaiting turn in games or group situations
- often blurts out answers to questions before they have been completed
- has difficulty following through on instructions from others
- has difficulty sustaining attention in tasks or play activities
- often shifts from one uncompleted activity to another
- has difficulty playing quietly
- often talks excessively
- often interrupts or intrudes on others
- often does not seem to listen to what is being said to him or her
- often loses things necessary for tasks or activities at school or at home
- often engages in physically dangerous activities without considering possible consequences

Having reviewed the technical criteria for the diagnosis of ADHD, along with a brief summary of Dr. Hanson's evaluation, let's look a little closer at some of the specific behaviors that he used to suggest the diagnosis of ADHD.

A Closer Look at Jake's Behavior

In talking to the Smiths, Dr. Hanson found that Jake had actually had shown some notable symptoms of hyperactivity as early as age three or four. They had hoped that he would "outgrow" them, and found many explanations or excuses for his behavior. They had suffered through many years of self-doubt, wondering if there were some new parenting tool or disciplinary method that could save the situation. It wasn't until they were near the end of their rope that they considered professional help.

Like so many parents, the Smiths had mistakenly felt that they should be able to manage Jake's behavior with discipline and love. They took his unmanageable behavior as a reflection on their abilities as parents. Their guilt was, at times, almost overwhelming. It took a great deal of courage to reach out to professionals for help.

ADHD often shows up first at school. It is here that children are required to conform, sit still, follow instructions, and do all the things that are impossible for them to do. Many teachers are now trained to notice symptoms of ADHD, though this is not always the case. At times these children are treated as emotionally disturbed, and inappropriate explanations are given for their behavior.

In Jake's case, the teacher's report showed that there had been trouble getting Jake to stay in his seat, cooperate with other students, and stay on task. If there was any unusual noise, Jake was the first one out of his seat to see what was happening. He could not seem to get organized, and often forgot, misplaced, or lost his schoolwork. What work he did complete was done carelessly, with many mistakes. Teachers reported that it was difficult to get Jake to focus for any length of time on a school assignment. He needed constant supervision.

Because of the extra attention that Jake required, and his poor social skills, he was developing increasing problems with his peers. He had difficulty sharing and was prone to angry outbursts when things did not go his way. He would impulsively say things that would irritate other children, and he seemed oblivious to the social consequences of this behavior. Because these symptoms occurred both at home and at school, it seemed that Jake's problems were not highly related to environment. Therefore, Dr. Hanson and the Smiths agreed that a medical evaluation would be in order. They chose their pediatrician because he already had a relationship with Jake.

MEDICAL CONSULTATION

Jake seemed at ease with his pediatrician, whom he had known for a number of years. The doctor's gentle, humorous style helped to create a more relaxed, nonthreatening atmosphere. He had read Dr. Hanson's report and was familiar with the concerns Jake presented to his parents and teachers. Nevertheless, he encouraged Mr. and Mrs. Smith, as well as Jake, to talk about what they felt was happening. The doctor reviewed his charts, and noted that there had been some behavioral concerns a few years back, but they had agreed to simply watch their development. Now, seeing Jake tug at his shoestrings and pick up objects in the office as he was talking to him certainly pointed to ADHD. He watched as the Smiths repeatedly tried to get Jake to respect the articles on his desk, only to have him violate established boundaries again and again.

The doctor decided to ask Jake a few questions. "Do you think you are any different than other kids, Jake?"

"No. Not really," Jake answered. "Well, I do get into more trouble than other kids, mostly from not sitting still. Sometimes I think I'm kind of dumb because I don't do as well on tests."

"Do you think you have trouble paying attention, Jake?" he asked.

"Yeah, I guess so," Jake replied reluctantly.

"Let me tell you a story," the doctor continued. "Sometimes doing well in school is not so much about how smart you are, but about your ability to pay attention. Did you know that some say Benjamin Franklin and Albert Einstein may have had the same kinds of trouble paying attention as you do?"

"You're kidding!" said Jake. "They were sure pretty smart."

"Yes," agreed the doctor. "The problem of Attention Deficit Hyperactivity Disorder is not related to intelligence. It has to do with the brain's ability to focus, plan, and order things in our minds."

Jake seemed satisfied for the moment. The doctor went on to explain that he would run a few tests to rule out a few other possibilities and get back to them. He performed several routine procedures during the appointment.

A week later they again met with the doctor and discussed his findings. There were no indications of any other physical or medical problems. He discussed with them some of the key facts that they should know about ADHD.

First, the pediatrician reassured the Smiths that their parenting had not caused Jake to have ADHD. The relational issues they were encountering with Jake were more a response to the ADHD, and they should stop blaming themselves. Having some facts to deal with reassured the Smiths.

THE ROLE OF THE BRAIN

The Smiths still had some technical questions that they wanted answered about what was happening within Jake to cause his inability to control his behavior. The doctor explained to them some of the theories about ADHD, but emphasized again that they did not know much about the "whys" of ADHD. Still, more is being learned all the time about causal factors and medical and behavioral treatment.

One theory is that children affected by ADHD have somehow received some form of subtle brain damage to the central nervous system before birth. One theory states that the frontal lobes of ADHD children may have been affected and are not performing their inhibitory functions. The frontal lobes are also involved in regulating attention, activity, planning ability, and emotional reactions. It is theorized that one of the functions of the frontal lobes is to allow a person to evaluate his or her behavior, what we know as self-awareness. The frontal lobes also tell a person when to start or stop a certain behavior.

While the "whys" of ADHD are still in their infancy, progress is rapidly being made. Imaging studies are giving us a hint at which portion of the brain is being affected in ADHD. Studies show that the prefrontal cortex, part of the cerebellum, seems to be smaller in children with ADHD. The right prefrontal cortex is involved in editing one's behavior, inhibiting behaviors, and planning activities.

The genetic factor in ADHD is very high also. Twin studies conducted by Helene Gjone and Jon M. Sundet of the University of Oslo found that there was a strong genetic correlation to developing ADHD. Why this is so is not clear. Nongenetic factors that have been linked to ADHD include premature birth, maternal alcohol and tobacco use, and exposure to high levels of lead in early childhood.

Dr. R.A. Barkley, director of psychology and professor of neurology at the University of Massachusetts Medical Center, has studied ADHD for many years and believes that impaired behavioral inhibition and self-control are the central deficits of this disorder. He believes that self-control, or the ability to delay one's initial response to an event, is a critical skill to performing any task. Developing the ability to perform "executive functions" such as planning an activity, deflecting distractions, and taking proper steps toward reaching desired goals are very important skills that are found difficult, if not impossible, by the ADHD child or adult.

Dr. Barkley has identified four executive functions that play a critical role in ADHD. Briefly stated they are: (1) having a working memory of the task, and holding that information in the mind while working on the task; (2) having self-directed speech to remind how to perform the task; (3) monitoring and controlling emotions while performing a task; and (4) reconstitution, or breaking down observed behaviors and combining the parts into new actions.

As the Smiths heard the various theories about ADHD, and the typical behaviors exhibited by ADHD children, they felt more at ease. While the disorder was serious and the prognosis guarded, at least there was a name for the problem that had plagued their family for years. It was not something that they were imagining, or some problem for which they needed to blame themselves. Somehow things seemed clearer and easier now that the problem was identified.

"A MATTER THAT BECOMES CLEAR CEASES TO CONCERN US."

—*Friedrich Wilhelm Nietzsche*

Clarity

MEDICAL INTERVENTIONS

After discussing theories for a while, the Smiths asked the all-important question: "What do we do now?" The doctor discussed with them several medications that had been found to be highly effective with ADHD children. With Dr. Hanson's psychological tools, medication could provide important support for managing Jake's ADHD behavior.

Not surprisingly, the Smiths were reluctant to have their son placed on medications to control his behavior. They asked the typical questions about the impact medication would have over time on their son. Although treatment with medication for ADHD/ADD has been shown to have a powerful effect on the disorder, it is not without problems. Medication, they were told, is not a cure and should not be used as the only treatment strategy. Additionally, medications sometimes have negative side effects, such as slowed growth and occasionally a tic disorder. These problems are often remedied by reducing the dosage or changing to a different medication. As the Smiths were given more factual information, their fears were calmed.

Jake's pediatrician discussed specific medications with Terry and Michael. Two commonly used stimulant medications are Methyphenidate (Ritalin) and Pemoline (Cylert); other medications are available, including Concerta and Adderall. The use of medications has been shown to reduce symptoms in approximately seventy-five percent of ADHD children. These medications generally increase attention span while decreasing impulsivity, overactivity, and destructive behaviors. With many children the effect of the medication is quite remarkable. The

Smiths thought that it was certainly worth trying.

The Smiths learned that some children with ADHD are also prescribed an antidepressant because of the secondary depression that sometimes comes with their continuing frustration over their failure to learn, social problems, and consequent low self-esteem. Jake did not show any symptoms of depression, but that would not be totally ruled out until later. For now, it was decided that one of the stimulants appeared to be the treatment of choice.

The Smiths agreed to try the medications. The next step was to persuade Jake that taking them would not make him "different" from his peers. They also had to do some talking to encourage him to enter into counseling with Dr. Hanson. There was still a lot of work left to be done.

MEETING WITH THEIR PASTOR

While Terry was against the idea, Michael felt that the situation was "bad enough" that their pastor should know what was happening in their family. Terry admitted that she hated to bring their "skeletons out of the closet."

"I just don't think this has anything to do with the pastor," Terry protested.

"How can you say that?" replied Michael. "This is tearing up our family and tearing us apart as well. Our pastor has been through many of our problems in the past, and I think we need his prayer and support now."

"You might be right," Terry said sadly. "How did we get to this point in our lives? It seems like things have gone from bad to worse. What are we doing wrong?"

Michael reached out to touch her hand as she began to cry. They stood in their living room and simply looked at one another for a moment.

"I don't know exactly what to say to you, Terry, except that God knows what we are going through and has experienced every emotion that we have felt. We're not bad people because this is happening to us."

"I would really like to believe that. I know inside that you are right, but I still have nagging doubts. Well, let's call Pastor Swanson and let him pray with us."

Terry and Michael met with their pastor and were met with warm, loving care. Their pastor had not experienced anything like this personally, but he was well acquainted with grief, remorse, and anger.

Pastor Swanson listened as they poured out their hearts over the events of the past several years. "I don't just want to give you platitudes, folks. There is no easy answer for what you are going through, and if I gave you one you would see right through it. But God can reach down and be your companion as you travel this tough road. Let's just pray that the therapists, teachers, and physicians will help you know how best to work with Jake to meet his troubles."

Together they prayed and wept. Things seemed better having their pastor in on their struggles and becoming part of the team.

BEHAVIORAL TREATMENT INTERVENTIONS

Terry and Michael felt like they had an appointment every day of the week. It was hard to carry on their normal jobs while caring for the needs of Jake. But it was also good to have a team of caring professionals around them.

Terry and Michael Smith had left their pediatrician's office feeling encouraged. They now had a name to give to their son's major problems and felt less blame for them. They also felt much relief knowing that Jake did not willingly defy their authority or try to act rebellious. They felt a renewed sense of compassion for him and vowed to get whatever help they could that might alleviate some of his problems.

Dr. Hanson met with the Smiths alone for a session to talk more about ADHD. He wanted to help them know what they could expect in the months ahead, and encouraged them to be an integral part of the treatment. Jake would also benefit from participating in the planning and structuring of whatever behavior program they would devise. They were told that perhaps the most important concept to remember was that these children function best in **an environment with clear limits and a consistent and predictable system of reinforcements and consequences.**

The Smiths were given a list of strategies to use with Jake. They were told that a comprehensive behavioral plan would be the most effective. It should include the following strategies:

1. Discipline must be simple, consistent, and have natural, logical consequences when rules are broken.

2. Encouragement is a more effective tool than punishment. Catch your child doing things well and praise him for it.

3. Make clear contracts with your child regarding his behavior. Make it clear which behaviors are acceptable and what the consequences will be for failure to abide by the agreed-upon rules.

4. Handle failures with a matter-of-fact attitude. Model calm and gentle behavior. Do not react emotionally to his negative behaviors.

5. Time-outs are often effective disciplinary tools with children. Find a neutral place in your home that can be used for time-outs.

6. In addition to praise, find other reinforcements to help your child strive to meet expectations. Again, keep the system simple, structured, and consistent.

7. Assist your child with planning by having a calendar posted on the refrigerator. Keep track of when assignments are due, and help him set a reasonable schedule for meeting deadlines.

8. Stay in touch with the school and coordinate assignments with them. Weekly progress reports are usually helpful.

9. Help your child develop social skills. This will help with the development of self-esteem, a critical issue with ADHD kids.

10. Take care to encourage your child to achieve all his potential. Believe in him. Maintain a vision for when he is too discouraged to see it for himself.

Dr. Hanson encouraged the Smiths to be willing to develop a team approach to Jake's treatment—a team that would include their family, pediatrician, pastor, and school personnel. They

> "VISION IS THE ART OF SEEING THINGS
> INVISIBLE."
>
> —*Jonathan Swift*

would need to coordinate services effectively for the best treatment results. Together they would target Jake's behavior in school, including his academic performance, social skills, and associated self-esteem issues. Family life would need to be structured and stable to support these goals.

It would be critical that the behavior modification system that they devised be supported and used both at home and at school. Jake might need a more structured and specialized classroom that already used behavior modification techniques. A behavioral program that used both positive reinforcement and punishment would be developed and used to support goals developed for Jake. The parents and teachers would be as important in the therapeutic process, if not more so, than the services offered by Dr. Hanson. It might be useful for the parents to participate in a support group with other parents in similar circumstances.

Finally, Dr. Hanson offered some rather sobering statistics about ADHD children. It was not what the Smiths wanted to hear, but it confirmed some of their suspicions. He told them that in roughly 50 percent of ADHD cases some of the symptoms persist into adulthood. Children whose symptoms persist into adolescence are at a high risk for developing conduct disorders and substance abuse problems. They are vulnerable to antisocial and other personality disorders, as well as prolonged learning problems. It was important that the Smiths were seeking help at this time and were willing to cooperate with a comprehensive plan of services. The family could make a valuable contribution in the treatment of Jake's ADHD.

Teaching a Chicken to Dance

A story is told about teaching a chicken to dance. I'm not sure why anyone would want to teach a chicken to dance, but the story may be helpful as we continue to learn about ADHD and its treatment.

It is actually possible, I am told, to teach a chicken to dance to certain choreographed steps. Much of the strategy involves rewarding the chicken each time it moves close to the desired behavior. The principles are similar to teaching any child to perform predetermined actions. In psychology we call this process *shaping*. The process involves reinforcing actions that approximate the desired outcome. The trick is to start simple, reinforcing each step, and work your way up to more complex tasks. Each step must be associated with the step preceding it. Given enough time, patience, and reinforcement, many complex behaviors can be learned.

Children with ADHD are good candidates for this kind of treatment regimen because of their difficulty in learning and remembering sequential steps. The greatest challenge with this process lies with the teacher or parents maintaining consistency and perseverance.

A major reason I like this treatment strategy is its emphasis on reinforcing positive behavior. Whenever working with children, it is best to avoid yelling or humiliating them. Try watching for behavior close to the desired outcome and reinforcing it. This is especially true for ADHD/ADD children, who may already be struggling with self-esteem.

ALTERNATIVE THERAPIES

Anyone involved in the treatment of ADHD has heard of, or explored, alternative therapeutic approaches to the problem. My goal here will be to introduce some optional ideas and let you explore them for their validity. Generally speaking, they are not mainstream ideas. This fact, in and of itself, does not make them invalid or not worth consideration.

One of the earliest "alternative" approaches to the treatment of ADHD is the Feingold diet, popularized by Dr. Ben Feingold. Dr. Feingold claimed that when children were placed on his diet, at least half showed marked improvement. Research conducted by the National Institute of Health has thoroughly researched the issue of additive-free diets and found that for the majority of children food additives play no role in the disorder.

Significant interest has also been given to sugar-free diets. Stories abound regarding the detrimental effect sugar has upon the ADHD child. However, studies have not proven sugar to have any significant adverse effects on the behavior of school-age children.

Vitamin therapy is another treatment modality used with some ADHD children. Again, there is apparently no definitive proof that megavitamin therapy is beneficial to these children.

Caution must also be given regarding the toxic effect of excessive vitamin dosages.

Herbal remedies have also been used with ADHD children. The American Academy of Child and Adolescent Psychiatry has suggested that there is no empirical evidence that these remedies are effective.

Having said this, it must be emphasized that you know your child better than others do and are in the best position to determine the effect of additives, sugar, and other alternative therapies on your child.

EMOTIONAL IMPACT OF ADHD ON CHILDREN

Children are often painfully aware that they are different from other children. They become aware, quite quickly, that adults are often angry with them for their failure to follow instructions and pay attention. Other children are perceived to receive preferential treatment. As one mother said, "I always feel mad at him." These children can sense the anger directed at them and it effects their self-esteem.

Unfortunately, because of the reactions of others to these children, they often develop other problems associated with their ADHD/ADD. They are often disliked by their peers and feel the rejection keenly. They often are treated differently by parents and teachers. They are treated as if they should be able to manage their behavior, when in fact it is, in large part, outside of their voluntary control. Because of these additional factors, children will need counseling to deal with the emotional aspects of the disorder.

EMOTIONAL IMPACT ON THE FAMILY

Perhaps enough has already been said about the incredible challenge of raising a special-needs child. Often isolated, guilt-ridden, and emotionally overloaded, parents are expected to make these children behave. When they misbehave in class, at church, or in the home, there is often the nagging doubt that they should somehow be able to control this conduct.

We have also mentioned that the ADHD child can wreak havoc in the emotional life of the family. It is not just the child who is affected, or just the parents. The entire family, including siblings, feel the impact of the ADHD child. Siblings come to resent this child. Parents prefer not to be around them. Marriage relationships are strained by the toll of caring for these children. Families feel a great weight when it comes to caring for children with this disorder.

Hopefully, if you are one of these parents, and have felt this sense of inadequacy, you are now feeling some relief. *You did not cause the problem, and you alone cannot fix it.* It is a biochemical, emotional, social problem that requires a multidisciplinary treatment approach. You are a critical member of the team of experts that must be called upon for the solution. There will be no quick fixes, no cures, and possibly no end to some aspects of the problem. Thus, given the nature of the problem, it will be important that you be kind to yourself, try to be patient, and seek as much support as you need.

What Else Parents Can Do

We know that being prepared for a situation enables us to enter that arena with more confidence. This applies to working with our ADHD children as well. There are several things that you, as parents, should know and do to enhance the possibility of success with your child.

1. Be proactive. Be informed about this disorder, various treatment strategies, and the role that you play in them. Learn all that you can about behavior-management strategies as well as medications.

2. Maintain collaboration with your team of professionals. You need them and they need you. Make sure that a professional evaluation is done and that appropriate medications are considered.

3. Participate in your child's learning at school. Be informed about your child's rights under two pertinent laws: Individuals with Disabilities Act and Section 504 of the Rehabilitation Act.

4. Take care of yourself. This is a marathon, not a sprint. Participate in parental support groups, eat properly, get enough sleep, and ask for relief as necessary.

ADULT ADHD

A final word about the longevity of ADHD is in order. For years it was believed and taught that children outgrow ADHD in their adolescence and early adulthood. Evidence is now surfacing that this is not necessarily the case. Adult ADHD, however, remains a controversial diagnosis. We are still in our infancy of learning about this phenomenon.

Current research suggests that approximately 50 percent of children with ADHD will have residual symptoms in adulthood. Typical symptoms for adults include inattention, restlessness, disorganization, and distractibility.

The discovery of ADHD symptoms in adulthood, of course, has brought both relief and discouragement. Many had hoped that they would grow out of the disorder and had been told that would be the case. The initial findings that ADHD can indeed have residual effects and can be treated with psychostimulant medications has brought needed relief.

SUMMARY

Unfortunately, by the time a child with ADHD has come to the attention of treatment professionals, the family and child may have been struggling for years. The school is often the first place where the depth of the problem is realized, although the parents and family have often suspected problems for years. Typically a negative course has been taken, from parental and teacher exasperation to peer rejection and abandonment. Many have labeled the child "hyperactive" in the most derogatory use of the term. The child feels this rejection and yet does not have the tools or skills, let alone the biochemical capability, to deal with these problems. He has been fighting an uphill battle and blaming himself all the way.

But the challenging path that has led to the doctor's office is just the beginning. A long journey remains. With the proper use of medications many of the symptoms can be managed, though a total "cure" should not be expected. There may be problematic traits that follow the child into adulthood, creating special needs even then.

There is, however, reason for hope. We are learning more about the origins and management of ADHD all the time. We are learning that a complete multidisciplinary approach can yield very positive results. If you suspect you are the parent of an ADHD/ADD child, you do not need to face this situation alone. There is a team of trained professionals ready to assist you in the care and training of your child. Reach out to them and insist upon receiving help. It is available to you. In this atmosphere your ADHD child can grow and develop to his fullest potential.

For Further Reading:

1. American Psychiatric Association. *Diagnostic and Statistical Manual of Mental Disorders—Fourth Edition.* Washington D.C., 1994.

2. Barkley, R.A. *Hyperactive Children: A Handbook of Diagnosis and Treatment.* New York: The Guilford Press, 1987.

3. Barkley, R.A. *Taking Charge of ADHD: The Complete, Authoritative Guide for Parents.* New York: Guilford Press, 1995.

4. Barkley, R.A. *Attention-Deficit Hyperactivity Disorder: A Handbook for Diagnosis and Treatment.* New York: Guilford Press, 1998.

5. Hinshaw, S. P. and Melnick, S. *Attention Deficits and Hyperactive Children.* Sage Publications: 1992.

6. Wender, P. *The Hyperactive Child, Adolescent and Adult: Attention Deficit Disorder Through the Lifespan.* Oxford University Press: 1987.